The Jamestown Storybook

By Carole Marsh

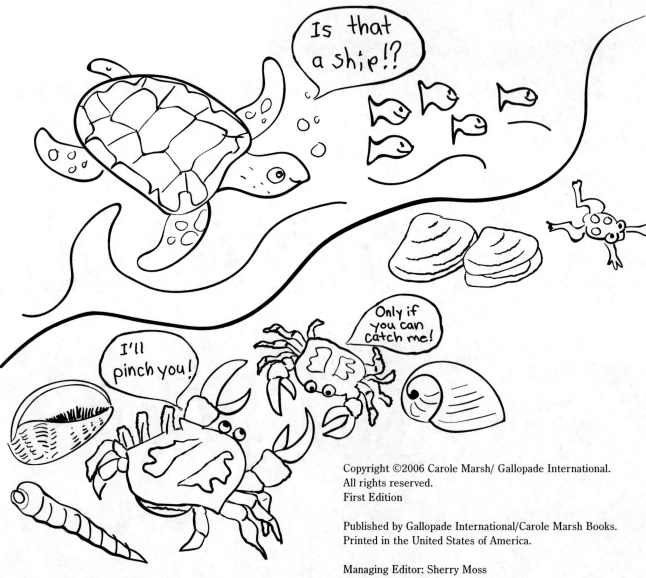

Published by Gallopade International/Carole Marsh Books.
Printed in the United States of America.

Managing Editor: Sherry Moss
Editorial Assistant: Janice Baker
Cover Design: Vicki DeJoy
Content Design: Steven St. Laurent, Line Creek Creative

Gallopade would like to acknowledge the APVA at Historic
Jamestowne and the Jamestown Yorktown Foundation for lending
us their expertise.

Gallopade is proud to be a member and supporter of these
educational organizations and associations:

American Booksellers Association
International Reading Association
National Association for Gifted Children
The National School Supply and Equipment Association
The National Council for the Social Studies
Museum Store Association
Association of Partners for Public Lands

A Word from the Author

Dear Reader,

Behind every historical event, there are stories to be told! People who lived, people who died, people who led the way, and people who quietly worked hard behind the scenes and made things happen in their own special way. People have made this country what it is today, and it all started in Jamestown!

The story of Jamestown is a story of triumph and tragedy. It's a wonder anyone survived when faced with disease, starvation, Indian attacks, and backbreaking work day after day! But they did it! Do you wonder what kind of friendships and conflicts they had? Do you wonder where they lived? Do you wonder what kind of games they played? Do you wonder about the words they spoke? These are the stories of Jamestown!

When I visited Jamestown a few years ago, I thought it was a beautiful place. I always say I'm a "fourth-grader forever," but that day, I acted like one by swinging on vines as thick as my arm…from trees that almost certainly shaded Captain John Smith and his men 400 years ago! I love experiences like that! I have thoroughly enjoyed investigating the stories of Jamestown, and hope you will have as much fun reading them!

Carole Marsh

Other Books in the Jamestown

Series

Carole Marsh Mysteries:

The Mystery at Jamestown,
First Permanent English Colony in America!

Carole Marsh Books:

Jamestown Trivia!
Fascinating
Facts for Kids

American Milestones:

Jamestown: America's First Permanent English Settlement

Jamestown Readers:

John Rolfe	Pocahontas
Queen Anne	Chief Powhatan
Christopher Newport	Captain John Smith
Thomas West, Lord De La Warr	

Plus!

Jamestown Mural

Table of Contents

of the Jamestown Storybook

The Virginia Company

An Invitation to a Strange "New World"

The 15th and 16th centuries were the Age of Discovery! It was a time when new lands were being explored with the promise of great riches and amazing adventure! The world's most powerful countries—including Spain, France, Portugal and England—were exploring the western hemisphere. What did they want? The answer was power, influence, and riches!

The new king of England, James I, wanted to establish colonies. In 1606, he granted a charter to the Virginia Company of London to establish an English colony in North America. Their first goal was money. They wanted to be the first to find the riches they had heard about from early explorers. But they had other goals as well. They also wanted to explore, build settlements, and convert the Virginia Indians to Christianity.

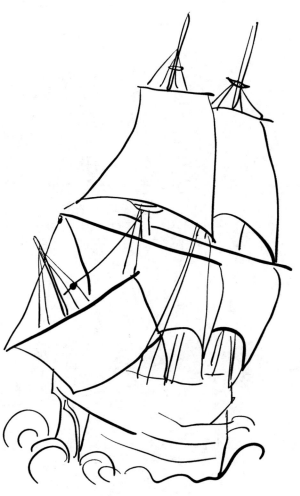

There were two types of members in the Virginia Company. Those who had money to invest but wanted to remain in England were called "adventurers." Those who wanted to settle in the new colony were called "planters."

Planters had to work for the Company for a set number of years. In exchange, they received a place to live, clothing, and food. At the end of his service, a planter was given a piece of land. Plus, he could get a share of the profit made by the Company. It was a risk, but one the planters were willing to take.

The Company also brought indentured servants to Virginia. They were usually required to work for seven years. This paid back the cost of their trip over to the colony.

On a cold winter day in December 1606, three ships funded by the Virginia Company set sail for North America. There were 144 people on board. The group included 39 crewmembers and four boys. Previous explorations proved that they were in for a real challenge!

Upon landing on the Virginia shore in the spring of 1607, the settlers knew their marching orders. They were to make a profit for the company! But they soon realized that just surviving in this strange new place was going to take all their energy! There was a fort to build, drinking water to find, and Indians to meet, communicate with, and work with. There were crops to plant, wood to cut, and animals to tend. And they met an enemy stronger than any other–disease!

While the first settlers struggled in Jamestown, the Virginia Company continued to look for more colonists. They needed to attract as many people as they could to make a profit! They spread the word about the excellent farming and opportunities in the new colony.

Despite their difficult life, the colonists did try to start small industries in Jamestown. They used the plentiful trees to make pitch and tar. They used corn to make beer. They tried their hand at glass-making. Unfortunately, the struggle to survive left little time for anything else!

Finally, a man named John Rolfe had an idea. He planted tobacco seeds from the West Indies in the fertile Virginia soil. His crops were healthy and abundant! He then learned how to cure the leaves until they were brown. He shipped the dried leaves back to England, where the British loved them! Finally, the Virginia Company had the profitable crop they needed!

The Virginia Company issued an invitation to ordinary people to move to a strange new world. If they could see the future, would they have gone? Would they have stayed back home in England? No, the invitation was accepted! It launched these brave travelers on a journey they would never forget! And it laid the foundation for the establishment of a new nation—the United States of America—the most powerful country in the world!

Along Came Three Ships

Allow me to introduce myself. My name is Discovery. You may have heard of me—I've become quite famous over the years! I am one of the ships that brought the very first colonists to Jamestown in 1607. You might want to sit down—I have quite a story to tell!

I was a bit concerned when I first heard what they wanted me to do! After all, I'm not a very big boat. I heard people describe me as "tiny!" But you know, I wasn't designed to carry people. I'm a cargo vessel!

Anyway, back to what I was saying. I just couldn't believe it when I heard I was going to be taking colonists all the way across the Atlantic Ocean! But my friends Susan Constant and Godspeed were going along so I figured we'd be all right. They are a bit bigger than me. Plus, the Susan Constant had Christopher Newport for her captain. He certainly knew his way around the high seas!

I felt a bit sorry for the 21 men jammed on board my deck. It was so crowded! I didn't have any cabins or any special place for them to sleep. They just had to grab a blanket and find a spot wherever they could. But it was just as bad on the other two ships! The Susan Constant carried 71 people, and the Godspeed had 52 folks on board. And remember—we carried food and supplies, too!

Unfortunately, our journey didn't start out so well. We were stuck off the coast of England for a month! The winds were just not filling my sails. Some storms came our way, too. I could hear some of the men arguing, and others were getting seasick.

Once we finally got on our way, we headed south to the Canary Islands off the coast of Africa. The warm waters felt sooooo good! Then we headed all the way across the Atlantic to the West Indies. My crew traded some knives and hatchets for fruits and vegetables. I know they liked the fresh food, but I didn't like the way they left the fruit peels all over my deck!

The last leg of our journey seemed endless. Finally, on April 26, we saw land! We sailed into a bay called Chesapeake and my crew dropped my anchor. I was so relieved. It had taken four months to get here!

Soon I had to say goodbye to my friends as they sailed back to England for supplies. I stayed behind to help the colonists explore the strange new land. Whew—could I tell you some stories! But we'll have to save that for another day.

The Voyage of the
Susan Constant, the Godspeed,
and the Discovery,
1606–1607

England [DEC. 1606–JAN. 1607]

EUROPE

NORTH AMERICA

Jamestown [MAY 14, 1607]

Virginia [APRIL 26, 1607]

Canary Islands [FEB. 1607]

AFRICA

West Indies

Atlantic Ocean

SOUTH AMERICA

Atlantic Ocean

Hispaniola

Mona & Monito [APR. 7–10]

Vieques [APR. 6]

Puerto Rico [APR. 6]

St. Croix? [APR. 4–5]

Nevis [MAR. 28–APR. 3]

Guadeloupe [MAR. 17]

Dominica [MAR. 24]

Caribbean Sea

Martinique [MAR. 23]

The *Susan Constant*

The *Godspeed*

Mud and Stud

Building a New Colony is Hard Work!

Have you ever used a hatchet to chop down a tree? It doesn't look like really hard work, but it is! Can you imagine cutting down enough trees to build a fort? Can you imagine dragging those trees by hand into position? Can you imagine digging a hole in the ground for the trees to stand? Can you imagine doing all that in the summer heat of Virginia? (And that was just the beginning!)

The Jamestown settlers did it all. They entered Virginia with the clothes on their backs, provisions, and tools. One of their first assignments: build a fort for safety!

The colonists decided on a triangular shape for their fort. It faced the river so they could see anyone coming toward them by water. They didn't waste any time, either! The 104 men and boys of Jamestown completed their fort just a month after coming ashore. They were men on a mission!

Once the walls were up, the colonists went to work on the public buildings. They included a storehouse, a church, and a guardhouse. The storehouse was watched constantly—after all, it held all their precious supplies! The church

served as a meeting
place. Soldiers slept in the guardhouse,
and stored their weapons there.

To make their own houses, the colonists used building methods they had learned
in England. Remember, building each structure meant chopping more wood,
stripping bark, pulling off branches...the work was endless!

The first Jamestown house builders used a technique called "mud and stud."
First, a sturdy frame was made from wood. Then, split saplings (young trees)
were lined up between the timbers to form a wall of studs. Finally, the studs were
covered with a type of paste made from clay, sand, straw, and water, known as
the "mud." Thatched roofs were made from plant materials like straw or reeds.
(Do you think they might have had a leak or two in a driving rain?)

After all that work, you won't believe what happened! In January of 1608, part
of the fort burned and had to be rebuilt. There was "no rest for the weary" in
Jamestown!

Captain *John Smith*

The Fearless Leader

When you read history, you will see that certain people stand out as leaders. They take charge, they make decisions, and they make things happen!

Captain John Smith was one of those people. He left home when he was 16 and became a soldier. While in present-day Romania, John was captured and made a slave! However, the sly, brave John Smith made a daring escape and traveled all the way back to England.

Always looking for adventure, John joined the Virginia Company expedition for Virginia. During the four-month journey, there were arguments among the passengers. The outspoken John Smith was right in the middle of many of them! He was arrested before the colonists ever reached Virginia. He was chained and kept below deck for 30 days.

When the colonists arrived in Virginia, they opened a sealed box that listed seven people chosen to govern the colony. John Smith's name was one of them.

The colonists faced many problems. The site they chose was swampy. They didn't have much fresh water. Sometimes the Powhatan Indians attacked the colonists. Disease began to spread.

John soon emerged as the colony's leader. He was not a person who wanted to be liked. He wanted to be feared and respected. Many of the colonists were not doing their share of the work. John saw that the colony would fail unless everyone helped out. He made an important rule—"He that will not work, shall not eat." Do you think he made his point nice and clear?

Powhatan Indians captured John Smith in December of 1607. He claimed that his life was saved by the chief's daughter, Pocahontas. By September of 1608, John was named president of the governing council in Jamestown. But things changed when he was badly wounded the following autumn. He sailed back to England for treatment and never returned to Jamestown.

While in England, John tried to convince more colonists to go to Virginia. In 1614, he sailed to the Maine and Massachusetts coastal areas. He named the region New England! When he returned to England, he wrote about his experiences in Jamestown. His books help us all understand the history of the first permanent English settlement in North America!

JOHN SMITH

Pocahontas

Little Girl with a BIG Personality

You have probably heard of Pocahontas! She was the young Powhatan Indian girl who is said to have saved the life of Captain John Smith in the early days of the Jamestown colony. Have you ever wondered about the rest of her life? Let's find out about it!

Pocahontas was the daughter of Powhatan. He was the main chief of more than 30 tribes. Pocahontas was probably born in 1595. She was named Matoaka, but got the nickname of Pocahontas because she was such a playful, fun-loving little girl. Pocahontas means "little mischievous one."

The famous legend about Pocahontas and Captain Smith tells of something that happened when Pocahontas was 10 or 11 years old. The Powhatan Indians captured Smith in December 1607. At first, Chief Powhatan was friendly to him. Then, suddenly, John was forced to the ground and the Indians stood over him with clubs. Pocahontas raced over to him and laid her head over his to save him! When Smith stood up, Chief Powhatan pledged that they were friends.

Some people believe that Pocahontas did not save Smith's life because she liked him. They think she saved him as part of a traditional ceremony the Powhatan Indians performed. Whatever the case, Pocahontas and Smith became friends after it happened.

Pocahontas visited Jamestown often. She came with Powhatans who brought food or furs to trade. She sometimes delivered messages from her father. She was curious about the English, and Smith enjoyed talking with her.

Smith describes her in his writings as a "lively girl." Her father Chief Powhatan must have loved her very much, because another colonist wrote that she was his "delight and darling." Wouldn't you have liked to meet her? She sounds like fun!

Pocahontas was kidnapped by a colonist named Captain Samuel Argall in 1613. He hoped to exchange her for English prisoners held by her father. Pocahontas became a Christian and took the name "Rebecca." She married a tobacco planter named John Rolfe and had a child named Thomas. Her marriage helped keep peace between the Powhatan Indians and colonists for many years.

Pocahontas traveled to England with her husband and was treated like a princess! Sadly, she got sick when she was just 22 years old and died before she could return to Virginia. She is remembered as an important peacemaker between the Powhatan Indians and the colonists!

Those Powhatans...
They Were Really Some Smart Cookies!

When the Jamestown colonists first met the Powhatan Indians, they didn't know anything about these natives living in Virginia. The colonists soon realized that they were dealing with a smart, hardworking, and advanced people. Here are some fast facts about the Powhatans!

▶ The Powhatan empire was huge! Chief Powhatan headed more than 30 tribes. Each tribe had a separate chief who swore loyalty to Powhatan.

▶ Powhatan was described by the English as tall and healthy. He never visited the English settlement. He made the English come to him, where he met them with 40 bodyguards, the finest of his 100 wives, priests, and counselors!

▶ The chiefs in Powhatan's empire were supposed to pay him 80 percent of all the copper, furs and crops they obtained. He kept it in a guarded storehouse. All the chiefs knew not to cheat Powhatan—he punished quickly and severely!

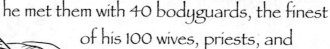

🔹 The Powhatans lived in villages that could include 100 homes. They lived in oblong houses called *yehakins*.

🔹 The tribes got their food through farming, hunting, fishing, and gathering nuts and berries.

🔹 Powhatan women worked very hard. They farmed and harvested the crops, as well as cooked, cleaned, gathered wood, and tended the animals.

🔹 The Powhatans made tools including hatchets, knives, drills, and arrows from stone and wood. Bones and antlers were used to make needles and fishhooks.

🔹 Powhatan men wore a breechcloth of animal skin and shirts of deerskin or a covering of turkey feathers. Their hair was shaved on the right side to keep from getting tangled in the bow while hunting. The hair on the other side was long, tied in a knot, and decorated with such things as deer antlers, shells, or rattlesnake rattles!

🔹 Powhatan women wore skirts. Married women wore their hair in long braids. Young girls shaved their heads on the front and sides. The rest of the hair was braided down their backs. (Sounds like the Powhatan version of a Mohawk!) Women also wore tattoos all over their body.

🔹 Powhatan babies were put on cradle boards until they were able to crawl. The baby and the board were sometimes laid flat, sometimes propped up, and sometimes hung on a tree if Mom was really busy!

There is Always Time For Fun
and Games!

Powhatan and colonial children worked hard! The work they did helped their families and their communities to survive.

Powhatan children learned their responsibilities from parents and other adults in their villages. Girls worked in the garden, cared for younger children, and helped prepare food. Boys learned how to hunt and fish. Hunting was a very important skill. Mothers would often test their boys' archery skills by tossing something into the air so they could shoot an arrow at it.

Colonial children had work to do, too. Boys would learn skills like hunting, carpentry, or blacksmithing. Girls might learn to be a seamstress.

Let the Games Begin!

But all work and no play is just no fun! Both the Powhatan and colonial children had time for their favorite games.

Powhatan boys played a type of football game. The girls often played with dolls made from cornhusks.

Colonial children had a few homemade toys. These might include a doll, a yo-yo, or a hobbyhorse. They enjoyed games like ninepins or quoits.

Ninepins is a lot like bowling, except the pins and ball are much smaller. It was played on the floor or on a table. Quoits was a very popular game. It was played by throwing rings at a stake (much like the game of horseshoes, which came from quoits!) Colonial children used whatever they could for rings, including strips of leather, pieces of rope, or willow branches made into a circle.

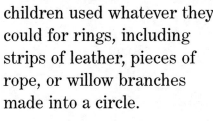

Jacob's Story

The first Africans arrived in Jamestown in 1619. They were captives on board a Dutch ship. The Dutch traded them for food! This could be one of their stories...

I remember that my heart was pounding. It looked as if things were going from bad to worse. We were Africans. We belonged in Africa! We had been stolen from our homes. We hated our captors! Then, people from another ship took us. One of my friends said they were Dutch. What did it matter...we knew we were in trouble.

I saw the Dutch men talking to other men on the shore. I heard them say the name of the town we had landed in—"Jamestown." I saw the Dutch men smile and take baskets of food from the men at Jamestown. Then our master marched all 20 of us off the ship. We stood there on the shore. Where were we now? What was going to happen to us?

The Jamestown men gave us clothes and allowed us to have a bath. It lifted my spirits but I was still afraid. They gave us something to eat. After that, one of the men sat us all down in a row. He pointed at each one of us and spoke one strange word to each of us. I realized that he was giving us new names. My name became Jacob.

We began to work for these strange new people...

I helped them plant and water their crops. I watched over the new plants and protected them from animals. There were so many creatures in this new world—furry ones that I'd never seen in Africa. They would run back into the forest after I chased them away. There were so many trees in this new world, too!

My friends and I knew that we were servants of these people. We knew we had no choice. But as we began to learn the language, we found out something that made us happy. These people would set us free after seven years! They explained that was their custom. They called us "indentured servants." I had something to hope for!

Now I am an old man and have seen many things. My friends and I were set free after our seven years of work. But the people in Virginia began to grow a plant named tobacco. They made a lot of money from it. They needed lots of help to grow it, so they brought in more Africans to help them. This time, the Africans were slaves for life.

It breaks my heart to watch the slaves work and work and work. I hope for a day—soon—where they will be set free.

What Happened to James Fort?

On May 14, 1607, the Virginia Company colonists landed on Jamestown Island. They built a fort and did their best to build a life. They fought against disease, starvation, and Indian attacks. It's a wonder they survived!

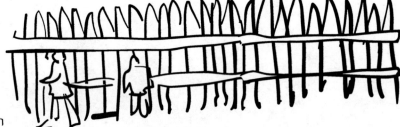

Have you ever wondered what happened to James Fort? Settlers eventually moved out of the fort to establish a "new town" of Jamestown to the east. There is not much said about James Fort after the 1620s.

Jamestown was the capital of Virginia until 1699. The statehouse burned to the ground that year, and Williamsburg became the capital in 1699. The land around Jamestown became the property of the two farming families by the 1750s.

During the American Revolution, a military post was located on Jamestown Island. In 1861, the landowner and his slaves built an earthen fort there to help block Union soldiers from moving up the James River.

Jamestown was owned by the Barney family in the late 1800s. They gave 22.5 acres of land to the Association for the Preservation of Virginia Antiquities (APVA). This group wanted to preserve Jamestown's 17th century church tower.

Archaeologists discovered in the mid-1990s that the remains of James Fort were indeed on the APVA property around the church tower! Historical archaeologists are finding new discoveries at the site every day!

And You Thought Trees Couldn't Talk!

Scientists, archaeologists, and historians are constantly trying to find out more about Jamestown. Why did so many people die? What was their life like? How did they live?

One excellent tool used by scientists to find out about the past is the tree. Trees have annual growth rings. Certain trees grow according to how much water they can absorb. Thick growth rings show years with lots of water. Thin growth rings show years of little water, or drought.

Some trees are really old, so they can help scientists look at weather patterns from centuries past! Bald cypress trees along the Blackwater River in southeastern Virginia have helped scientists study the history of Jamestown.

According to the Virginia bald cypress trees, the Jamestown colonists had some bad luck! They arrived during a very long drought. It lasted from 1606 to 1612. Drought means less water to drink and less water for crops.

Do you think you'll look at a huge old tree a little differently the next time you see one? It's not just a tree, it's a history lesson!

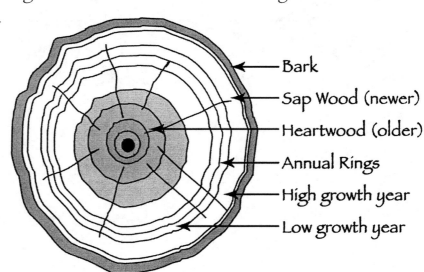

— Bark
— Sap Wood (newer)
— Heartwood (older)
— Annual Rings
— High growth year
— Low growth year

Can You Dig It?

Archaeologists Unearth New Answers to Old Questions

What have archaeologists found as they dig through the remains of James Fort? Lots of goodies that tell us a great deal about how the colonists lived in Jamestown!

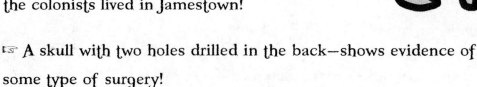

☞ A skull with two holes drilled in the back—shows evidence of some type of surgery!

☞ A well that may be the one Captain John Smith ordered to be dug in 1609. He was looking for fresh water since the marshy water around the fort was unhealthy.

☞ Animal bones that show evidence of what food the early colonists ate. They dined on fish, turtles, rays, birds, oysters, and raccoons, plus beef and pork from England.

☞ Breastplates and helmets

☞ Beads to trade with Indians

☞ Surgical tools and medical storage jars

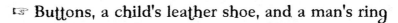

☞ Buttons, a child's leather shoe, and a man's ring

☞ Game pieces and dice

☞ English tobacco pipe

☞ A brass cymbal from a tambourine

☞ A musical instrument similar to a recorder

Only The Rats Know For Sure!

Almost 90 percent of the colonists in Jamestown died during the winter of 1609-1610. It was called "The Starving Time." Some scientists think rats carrying the plague may have been the reason! Two clues:

🐀 There is evidence that colonists were eating black rats, which could have only come from England. Those rats often carried the plague!

🐀 Many of the bodies were buried in a big hurry! This is usually done when there is a contagious disease present.

Rats or no rats—this is another history mystery with no clear answer!

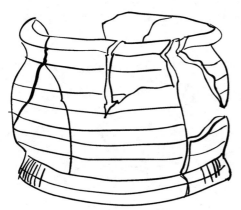

Tidewater Trivia

Look a Little Closer
at Jamestown with Tons of Terrific Trivia!

The English believed that the natives were actually born as white people and then their skin changed colors as an effect from the dyes they used to decorate themselves and ward off mosquitoes!

Along with the colonists and crew, the three ships held provisions, tools, and parts for a smaller boat that would be assembled in Virginia and used for inland exploration!

In 1607, Chief Powhatan's empire covered all of modern-day eastern Virginia and spread down to the Virginia-North Carolina line!

Christopher Newport sailed back to England after dropping off the colonists. The colonists sent letters back with him but each letter was screened to make sure that it did not say anything negative about the colony!

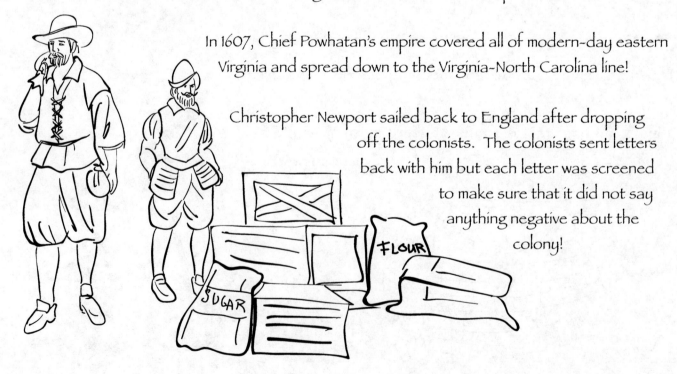

John Smith dreamed of going overseas ever since he was a young boy but his father stopped him. When he was 16 or 17, his father died and John was free to go out to sea!

The natives built their own canoes and it was not an easy task. First, they had to hollow out a large log by partially burning it and then form the shape by scraping the log inside and out with oyster shells and stone tools!

When the colonists finally came into Chesapeake Bay after their journey across the ocean, they stopped and raised a cross, thankful that they had arrived!

John Smith made remarkably accurate maps and charts of the Virginia coastline!

A dependable source of food for the Native Americans and settlers was the Virginia white-tailed deer!

It wasn't until the fall of 1609 that the settlers harvested their first crop of corn!

Most of the time, even when crops of corn were needed, tobacco would be planted instead because it was the money-maker of the colony! In fact, the demand for tobacco was so high that it was even planted in the streets!

In the 17th century, the time of the Jamestown colony, people ate using knives, spoons, and hands. The fork was not in common use by Englishmen until more than 100 years after the founding of Jamestown!

The Powhatan Indians treasured copper like the English treasured gold. Judging by the amount of copper scraps that have been found by archaeologists, a jeweler in Jamestown must have been busy making copper items to trade with the Indians!

What Do You Call That?

Colonists came across many things—animals, plants, food— in the New World they had never seen before. So how did they know what to call them? Colonists often asked the Native Americans, and blended those new words into their language.

The Powhatan Indians were part of the Algonquian language group. Here are some examples of Algonquian words in our English language today:

moose	opossum	raccoon
skunk	muskrat	squash
succotash	moccasin	papoose
pecan	toboggan	tomahawk
hickory	caucus	

Many place names and state names are Algonquian in origin, too!

Chesapeake ("great shellfish bay")
Connecticut ("long river place")
Illinois ("men" or "warriors")
Mississippi (from Algonquian word "Messipi")
Missouri ("river of the big canoes")
Wyoming ("large prairie place")

Expand Your Vocabulary With Powhatan

Words!

Have some fun bringing some Powhatan words into your life. Would you like a grilled "ootun" sandwich? How about closing your "muskins" before you go to sleep? And make sure you kiss your "kowse" goodnight before you go to bed!

English	Powhatan
apple	maracah
arm	mese
arrow	attonce
ball	aitowh
butterfly	manaang-gwas
canoe	aquiontan
cheese	ootun
child	nechaun
dog	attemous
eat	mecher
eyes	muskins
father	kowse
friend	netab
hello, friend	wingapo
fire	pokatawer
goose	kehunge

Happy Birthday Jamestown!

Jamestown celebrates its 400th anniversary in 2007! The party really began when 105 brave souls and their crew set sail from the comforts of England in December 1606. What an adventure—and what a country!—waited for them on the other side of the ocean!

One highlight of the anniversary celebration will be a replica of the Godspeed sailing into six eastern ports. Another will be a "National Teach-In" broadcast to every school in America!

Other events will recognize the roles played by African Americans and Native Americans in the story of Jamestown. Fascinating artifacts will bring Jamestown to life at the Archaearium in Historic Jamestowne, site of the original James Fort!

What a great time to be a history student in America!